This book
belongs to

_____

More Little Lessons for Life

Written and Illustrated by
Kathy Arbuckle

BARBOUR
PUBLISHING, INC.

© MCMXCVII by Barbour Publishing, Inc.

ISBN 1-57748-286-7

Scripture quotations are from the KING JAMES VERSION of the Bible.

Published by Barbour Publishing, Inc.
    P.O. Box 719
    Uhrichsville, Ohio 44683
    http://www.barbourbooks.com

Member of the
Evangelical Christian
Publishers Association

Printed in China.

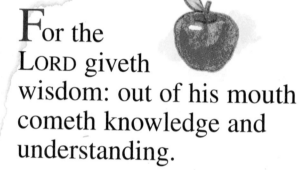

For the LORD giveth wisdom: out of his mouth cometh knowledge and understanding.

Proverbs 2:6

*For
Christina
and her
sunshine
smile.*

There is that speaketh like the piercings of a sword: but the tongue of the wise is health.

Proverbs 12:18

When someone says mean words to you it makes you feel bad, doesn't it? Your feelings are hurt and sometimes you might even cry. But when somebody says nice things to you and tells you good things, things they know will help you, that makes you happy. You feel good when you know people care about you and that they are there whenever you need them. Use your words to make others happy and God will be glad, too.

Bible Wisdom for Preschoolers

In the way of righteousness is life: and in the pathway thereof there is no death.

Proverbs 12:28

Imagine a pathway that leads to a beautiful city where the streets are paved with gold. The King who rules over that city is loving and very kind to all of His subjects. The people of this city wear crowns of gold with jewels and are never hungry or sad or sick. They live forever in this wonderful place. This is what God has for you when you follow Him and obey Him. When you believe in God's Son, Jesus, you will be walking on the pathway to heaven and life forever with the loving King.

Bible Wisdom for Preschoolers

The soul of the sluggard desireth, and hath nothing: but the soul of the diligent shall be made fat.

Proverbs 13:4

One day Kevin saw a toy dump truck at the toy store. He did not have enough money to buy it, so he asked his parents if he could do extra jobs to earn the money. It took some time and some hard work, but soon he had enough money to buy the shiny, new truck. Because Kevin was willing to work extra, he was able to get what he wanted. If he had been lazy, do you think he would have been able to buy his new toy?

Bible Wisdom for Preschoolers

There is that maketh himself rich, yet hath nothing: there is that maketh himself poor, yet hath great riches.

Proverbs 13:7

Long ago, King Solomon was the richest man in the world. He had so many jewels that he could never wear them all. His stables were filled with many fine horses and he lived in a grand palace. However, these riches did not make him happy. He was only truly happy when he was loving God with his whole heart. Even if King Solomon did not have a single penny, he still would have been happy as long as he loved and obeyed God. God's love is the greatest treasure you can have.

He that walketh with wise men shall be wise: but a companion of fools shall be destroyed.

Proverbs 13:20

Amy and Jennifer are very best friends. They both like to play with dolls and toy horses. Blue is their favorite color and they both like the same flavor of ice cream. But most important, they both love God. The two friends like to do what is right and share the love of God with each other and with their friends and families. Their friendship grows as they learn more and more about the Lord together.

What can God teach you today?

Bible Wisdom for Preschoolers

He that is soon angry dealeth foolishly.

Proverbs 14:17

Have you ever heard that someone has a "bad temper"? That means that the person gets very mad very easily. Do you like to be around somebody like that? It hurts your feelings when a person yells at you and is grumpy towards you. Being angry usually does not solve any problems, but instead makes them worse. God tells us not to have a bad temper, but to use kind words. He knows that is the best way to work out a problem.

Bible Wisdom for Preschoolers

A sound heart is the life of the flesh: but envy the rottenness of the bones.

Proverbs 14:30

Justin had a blue bicycle with training wheels. But Marty had a new, red bike with a headlight. Justin wished that he had Marty's bike instead of his. He was sad all the time because he thought the bike he had was not good enough. Justin was jealous. Soon he realized that God had given him his bicycle and that he should be thankful for it. Justin stopped wasting his time feeling bad and soon was out with Marty. They rode their nice bikes and had fun together. That made God happy.

Bible Wisdom for Preschoolers

He that oppresseth the poor reproacheth his Maker: but he that honoureth him hath mercy on the poor.

Proverbs 14:31

There are many poor people in the world who don't have much of anything. God's Son, Jesus, cares about the poor and told us to care about them, too, because He loves them. It pleases God when He sees you share with someone who might not have what you have. Besides, it is much more fun to fly a kite with a friend than to fly it all by yourself!

What can God teach you today? 23

A soft answer turneth away wrath: but grievous words stir up anger.

Proverbs 15:1

Kaitlyn wanted her puppy, Goldie, to come to her, so she shouted, "Goldie!" in a loud voice. The dog was afraid and did not come. Kaitlyn became angry and yelled louder at the frightened puppy. The little dog ran farther away. Finally, Kaitlyn thought, "How would Jesus call my doggie?" Sweetly, with a gentle voice, Kaitlyn called her puppy. Goldie's tail began to wag and she ran right into Kaitlyn's waiting arms for a loving hug. People like soft words, too, because they make love grow.

The eyes of the LORD are in every place, beholding the evil and the good.

Proverbs 15:3

Did you know that God is everywhere all of the time? He is so big and so awesome that He can be all over the universe at the same time. That is a good thing to think about as you go through your day. Always remember that God is right there to help you make good decisions and do the right things. We want to please God with everything we do and say all the day long.

What can God teach you today?   27

Bible Wisdom for Preschoolers

The L<small>ORD</small> is far from the wicked: but he heareth the prayer of the righteous.

Proverbs 15:29

Nathan's great-grandma lives far away in another state. It is too far to visit by car, but the telephone lets them talk together as if they lived very close. Every Saturday morning, Nathan's great-grandma calls to talk to him. She likes to be able to tell him that she loves him. Your love for God makes you close to Him and when you are close to Him, He will hear your prayers. You can talk to Him anytime without even having to use the telephone!

Bible Wisdom for Preschoolers

How much better is it to get wisdom than gold! and to get understanding rather to be chosen than silver!

Proverbs 16:16

It is better to have wisdom and do what is right than to have all of the money in the world. Would God be happy if you were very rich, but you did not love Him? He would rather have your love even if you were the poorest of poor. You are more precious to Him than all the diamonds in the world! Knowing God and doing what He says is worth far more than the greatest treasures of gold and silver.

Bible Wisdom for Preschoolers

The highway of the upright is to depart from evil: he that keepeth his way preserveth his soul.

Proverbs 16:17

Imagine you are standing on a road trying to decide which way to go. If you go one way, the road leads to a smelly, dark garbage dump. But if you travel on that road the other way, it will lead you to a wonderful place where the air is filled with sweet music and laughter, and bright light shines all around you. Which way would you go? God says you should choose the good way, the way that goes far away from evil. As you travel with Him He will lead you and keep you safe in His love.

Bible Wisdom for Preschoolers

Pleasant words are as an honey-comb, sweet to the soul, and health to the bones.

Proverbs 16:24

Brianne's favorite fruit is juicy watermelon. She likes the sweet taste and how it crunches when she takes a bite. God made the watermelon so it is full of vitamins and other healthy things to help Brianne grow up big and strong. The Bible says that nice words are sweet. They are good for us to say and good for us to hear, too. Pleasant words help us to be healthy, happy children of God.

Bible Wisdom for Preschoolers

A friend loveth at all times, and a brother is born for adversity.

Proverbs 17:17

Amanda and Isabel are best friends. They do everything together. But when Amanda broke her leg falling off her trampoline, she could not go outside to play anymore until her leg healed. That didn't bother Isabel. She came over every day to visit her friend Amanda and play with her. Amanda had so much fun that she forgot all about her broken leg. God wants us to be good friends ALL of the time, in bad times and good.

The name of the LORD is a strong tower: the righteous runneth into it, and is safe.

Proverbs 18:10

Long ago, during Bible times, there were places called "cities of refuge." If someone was in trouble with another person, they could run to one of these cities and be safe. No one could come after them to hurt them as long as they stayed in that city of refuge. God is like a city of refuge. When you are afraid you can talk to Him and He will protect you like a strong tower. God is mightier than anyone or anything. He will be your safe place.

Bible Wisdom for Preschoolers

A man that hath friends must shew himself friendly: and there is a friend that sticketh closer than a brother.

Proverbs 18:24

Michael loved to go fishing. He went many, many times to the same pond, but never caught a fish. After a while fishing wasn't fun anymore. One day a new neighbor boy asked Michael if there were any good places to fish nearby. The two boys went together once, twice, three times, four times to the pond. They never did catch any fish, but they built a wonderful friendship that lasted their whole lives long. To have a friend you have to be a friend.

Bible Wisdom for Preschoolers

The sluggard will not plow by reason of the cold; therefore shall he beg in harvest, and have nothing.

Proverbs 20:4

Once there was a farmer who was lazy. On sunny days he might do a little work in his field if he felt like it, but if it was at all cold, he would not work at all. Time went by. Spring and summer were gone and it was harvesttime. All of the farmer's neighbors were harvesting their crops and storing food for the winter, but the lazy farmer did not have any crops to harvest. He was very hungry. The Bible says that if we are willing to work, we will earn what we need to live.

Bible Wisdom for Preschoolers

Who can say, I have made my heart clean, I am pure from my sin?

Proverbs 20:9

Benjamin likes to help wash the dishes. Now if no one washed those dishes, would they get clean all by themselves? No, they wouldn't. Someone has to get the dish soap and water and scrub them. When you do something bad you are like the dirty dishes. You can't clean away your sin by yourself. You have to be sorry and ask God to forgive you and wash away your sin. And just like the very best dishwasher, He will make you sparkling clean and pure!

What can God teach you today?   45

Bible Wisdom for Preschoolers

Say not thou, I will recompense evil; but wait on the LORD, and he shall save thee.

Proverbs 20:22

One summer day at the beach Luke and Zachary were building sand castles. Zachary was driving his toy dump truck too fast and knocked down Luke's sand castle. Luke became angry and wanted to go knock down Zachary's sand castle, but he remembered that God says not to "get even" with anyone. God will deal with that person Himself. It is not your job. After all, God's ways are perfect. He knows best what to do.

Every word of God is pure: he is a shield unto them that put their trust in him.

Proverbs 30:5